FINALLY FOCUSED

LASER

CONCENTRATION

Learn The Trick To Become Incredibly Productive In Everything You Do

Fred Park

Table of Contents

Chapter 1:

6 Steps To Focus On Growth

Growth is a lifelong process. We grow every moment from the day we are born until our eventual death. And the amazing thing about growth is that there is no real limit to it.

Now, what exactly is growth? Well, growing is the process of changing from one state to another and usually, it has to be positive; constructive; better-than-before. Although growth occurs equally towards all directions in the early years of our life, the rate of growth becomes more and more narrowed down to only a few particular aspects of our life as we become old. We become more distinctified as individuals, and due to our individuality, not everyone of us can possibly grow in all directions. With our individual personality, experiences, characteristics, our areas of growth become unique to us. Consequently, our chances of becoming successful in life corresponds to how we identify our areas of growth and beam them on to our activities with precision. Let us explore some ways to identify our key areas of growth and utilize them for the better of our life.

1. Identify Where You Can Grow

For a human being, growth is relative. One person cannot grow in every possible way because that's how humans are—we simply cannot do every thing at once. One person may grow in one way while another may grow in a completely different way. Areas of growth can be so unlike that one's positive growth might even seem like negative growth to another person's perspective. So, it is essential that we identify the prime areas where we need to grow. This can be done through taking surveys, asking people or critically analyzing oneself. Find out what lackings do you have as a human being, find out what others think that you lack as a human being. Do different things and note down where you are weak but you have to do it anyway. Then, make a list of those areas where you need growing and move on to the next step.

2. Accept That You Need To Grow In Certain Areas

After carefully identifying your lackings, accept these in your conscious and subconscious mind. Repeatedly admit to yourself and others that you lack so and so qualities where you wish to grow with time.

Never feel ashamed of your shortcomings. Embrace them comfortably because you cannot trully change yourself without accepting that you need to change. Growth is a dynamic change that drags you way out of your comfort zone and pushes you into the wild. And to start on this endeavor for growth, you need to have courage. Growth is a choice that requires acceptance and humility.

3. Remind Yourself of Your Shortcomings

You can either write it down and stick it on your fridge or just talk about it in front of people you've just met—this way, you'll constantly keep reminding yourself that you have to grow out of your lackings. And this remembrance will tell you to try—try improving little by little. Try growing.

It is important to remain consciously aware of these at all times because you never know when you might have to face what. All the little and big things you encounter every day are all opportunities of growth. This takes us to the fourth step:

4. Face Your Problems

Whatever you encounter, in any moment or place in your life is an opportunity created: an opportunity for learning. A very old adage goes: "the more we learn, the more we grow". So, if you don't face your problems and run away from them, then you are just losing the opportunity to learn from it, and thus, losing the opportunity of growing from it. Therefore, facing whatever life throws at you also has an important implication on your overall growth. Try to make yourself useful against all odds. Even if you fail at it, you will grow anyway.

5. Cross The Boundary

So, by now you have successfully identified your areas of growth, you have accepted them, you constantly try to remind yourself of them and you face everything that comes up, head on—never running away. You are already making progress. Now comes the step where you push yourself beyond your current status. You go out of what you are already facing and make yourself appear before even more unsettling circumstances.

This is a very difficult process, but if you grow out of here, nothing can stop you ever. And only a few people successfully make it through. You create your own problems, no one might support you and yet still, you try to push forward, make yourself overcome new heights of difficulties and grow like the tallest tree in the forest. You stand out of the crowd. This can only be done in one or two subjects in a lifetime. So make sure that you know where you want to grow. Where you want to invest that much effort, and time, and dedication. Then, give everything to it. Growth is a life's journey.

6. Embrace Your Growth

After you have crossed the boundary, there is no turning back. You have achieved new heights in your life, beyond what you thought you could have ever done. The area—the subject in which you tried to develop yourself, you have made yourself uniquely specialized in that particular area. You have outgrown the others in that field. It is time for you to make yourself habituated with that and embrace it gracefully. The wisdom you've accumulated through growth is invaluable—it has its roots deeply penetrated into your life. The journey that you've gone through while pursuing your growth will now define you. It is who you are.

As I've mentioned in the first line, "growth is a lifelong process". Growth is not a walk in the park, It is you tracking through rough terrains—steep heights and unexplored depths for an entire lifetime. Follow these simple yet difficult steps; grow into the tallest tree and your life will shine upon you like the graceful summer sun.

Chapter 2:

Trust The Process

Today we're going to talk about the power of having faith that things will work out for you even though you can't see the end in sight just yet. And why you need to simply trust in the process in all the things that you do.

Fear is something that we all have. We fear that if we quit our jobs to pursue our passions, that we may not be able to feed ourselves if our dreams do not work out. We fear that if we embark on a new business venture, that it might fail and we would have incurred financial and professional setbacks.

All this is borne out of the fear of the unknown. The truth is that we really do not know what can or will happen. We may try to imagine in our heads as much as we can, but we can never really know until we try and experienced it for ourselves.

The only way to overcome the fear of the unknown is to take small steps, one day at a time. We will, to the best of our ability, execute the plan that we have set for ourselves. And the rest we leave it up to the confidence that our actions will lead to results.

If problems arise, we deal with it there and then. We put out fires, we implement updated strategies, and we keep going. We keep going until we have exhausted all avenues. Until there is no more roads for us to travel, no more paths for us to create. That is the best thing that we can do.

If we constantly focus on the fear, we will never go anywhere. If we constantly worry about the future, we will never be happy with the present. If we dwell on our past failures, we will be a victim of our own shortcomings. We will not grow, we will not learn, we will not get better.

I challenge each and every one of you today to make the best out of every situation that you will face. Grab fear by the horns and toss them aside as if it were nothing. I believe in you and all that you can achieve.

Chapter 3:

Taking Action Is The Only Cure To Laziness

Action is the key to manifesting your dreams into reality.

First it must be built in the mind,

Then the body must take action to build it in the world.

You can't get going until you get going.

Laziness is holding you back.

You can't start successful,

but you can't be successful until you start.

Laziness is a sign of low self-esteem.

You don't do it because you don't believe you can.

You fear taking a leap of faith that is necessary for your success.

Take action towards the goal,

however small the progress is.

Reading a book on the subject for an hour a day,

exercising for an hour a day

will both bring you closer to your physical and emotional goals.

Most people underrate themselves.

What if all people were similar and could achieve similar results with similar effort?

Think about that.

Is that not reality?

If we agree it is, we have all sold ourselves short and it becomes clear we could be far more.

People would not be lazy if they knew they could do it for sure.

The truth is you have as much chance of being successful as Richard Branson or Opera Winfrey.

Andrew Carnegie, founder of U.S steel who was one of the richest people in history started as a poor Scottish mill worker.

He also gave away all his wealth in old age through philanthropy.

An important example of character for anyone.

Opportunity was a lot harder to find back then.

Your odds are far better today.

He had to sail across the world and spend decades building a company from nothing.

Today it is entirely possible to become successful without even leaving your home.

From your phone you can conduct business worldwide.

Laziness is simply a symptom of low faith in one's self.

As Henry Ford famously said.

" Weather you think you can, or think you can't , you are right.".

I believe this to be as true today as it was then.

The result is totally dependent on what you think.

If you think you can't, that is the problem.

The symptom is laziness and the result is nothing.

Not even failure, because failure would require effort and laziness is the lack of effort.

The curse of laziness is far worse than failure.

Those who fail can hold their heads high knowing they tried.

Those who fail by default due to laziness will taste the sour taste of true regret,

never knowing if they could have won because they never played.

Action is the only cure for laziness.

By taking the first step towards the goal,

you will see that this step brings progress.

It will motivate you to take the next step,

building momentum towards your goal.

Laziness is linked to self-esteem and your beliefs.

It can be overcome when you change your believes about yourself and your situation.

Take the first step of action when you don't feel ready is the leap of faith.

Without summoning the courage to take this leap we cannot fly.

Just as in nature,

if you were to base jump off a cliff,

your suit does not allow you to glide immediately,

first you must drop so the wind can catch your suit.

It's just the same in life.
As you take your leap,
things will often get worse before they get better.
To help the wind catch your suit you must continue to take action away from the cliff, because if you stay still and hit the rocks your dream will not catch the wind and die.

Keeping moving always
Look for the next step and continue towards the beautiful flight ahead.
Keeping in mind your inner concept of the dream,
of soaring on life's breeze,
living the high life with ease.

If the why for your end result is big enough,
it will give you the courage to take the leap and withstand the drop.

Always with the most magnificent image of your future life at the forefront of your mind,
keep unwavering faith that this is going to happen for you.

Through taking constant action,
having a burning desire for success,
there will be no room for laziness in your life.
Once you have taken the leap and endured the drop,
nothing will stop you from gliding from success to success.
But you must act now for success waits for no one.

Chapter 4:

BE CONSISTENT, NOT PERFECT

It's often drilled into our heads that we have to be **great** at everything we do. It sounds like a lot of pressure, right? Well, what if the key wasn't in being great but simply showing up all the time, over and over?

Lasting progress isn't about being consistently great; it's about being great at being consistent. That means, instead of focusing on doing things perfectly, you simply focus on just the doing and getting better as you progress. When we focus on being consistent, we give ourselves more of an opportunity for greatness.

We're constantly seeing others online who are seemingly achieving greatness overnight—leaving us feeling stuck. But what if i told you that the true power is in the process?

When we aim for consistency over perfection, these are the benefits:

1. **You're taken more seriously by those around you**

you can tell people until you're blue in the face what you *want* to do, but if you don't do it, they'll stop listening. However, if you show up every day and make a consistent effort, you'll be synonymous with what you're putting out there. Others will see from your actions that you're passionate about what you do or believe in.

2. **You'll make progress**

how many times have you prolonged doing something until it became practically nonexistent because you kept waiting for it to be perfect? It was a hard pill to swallow, but i found out that my fear archetype was the procrastinator a few months ago. I've always considered myself a perfectionist, and i find out procrastination is one of our key traits. We tweak things repeatedly, hoping to make them perfect, and end up never actually taking action. When we show up consistently, despite how perfect something may or may not be, we increase the possibility of progress.

By bringing more consistency into our lives, we'll have the opportunity to see true change in our circumstances. When we harp on perfection, it can often stunt our ability to grow. So, how do you become more consistent?

First, understand that you might mess up. And that's okay.

The biggest thing holding us back from being more consistent and instead relying on perfection is that we're afraid of making mistakes. When we mess up, we feel discouraged, and a way of protecting ourselves is by trying to control the outcome. So we wait until the time is perfect instead of taking the risk.

Allow yourself the space to be brave with your life. When faced with that fear, remind yourself that it's okay to make mistakes. To help, try reciting mantras like, "i may stumble, but i'll continue to learn and get better along the way."

A small step is always better than no step at all

The most beneficial thing we can do for ourselves if we ever want to see change is to take action. Whether big or small, you are putting yourself out there, and doing the work consistently adds up. When we settle into the comfort of perfection, we stifle our potential.

So today or tomorrow, take one small action that will help move you in the direction you seek. And after that, do another small thing.

Along the way, praise your small wills and honor your process. With time and a steady effort, the things you desire will begin to manifest themselves.

Chapter 5:

Stay Focused

A razor sharp focus is required to bridge the gap

between our vision and our current circumstances.

Stay focused on the vision we want,

despite the current reality.

It's challenging to believe you will be rich when you are poor,

healthy if you are sick,

but it is necessary to achieve that vision.

Focus on the desired result.

Focus on the next step towards that goal.

Without focus on these elements there can be no success.

Stay focused on the positive elements,

solutions over problems.

The expected reward over the fear, loss and pain along the way.

What we focus on will become.

Therefore we have to maintain our eyes on the prize.

Be results driven.

Always focus on bringing that result closer.

Focus on what your grateful for.

Gratefulness brings more of that into your life.

Focus on problems on the other hand brings more problems.

If we focus on a big goal today,

we might not be ready yet,

but we will become ready on the way.

Commit to the necessary changes you know you need.

Get ourselves ready for that goal.

So many never act simply because they don't know how.

They don't feel ready.

We can achieve nearly anything if we focus on it.

Think carefully about what you focus on.

It is critical to both your success and failure.

Know exactly what you want.

See the odds of a successful happy life increase by unfathomable amounts.

How can we be happy and successful if we never define what that is?

It's not about what you are, or what you were in the past.

It is all about what you are becoming and want to become.

We cannot let circumstances or the world decide that.

We must use our free will and decide who and what we will become and

focus fully on that.

Wishing, succumbing to the days whim, will never bring lasting success.

Success requires serious commitment and focus on that outcome.

Exude a fanatical level of focus.

Be exuberated in the pursuit of success.

The most successful often focus on work for over 100 hours per week. They give up most social interaction and even sleep to make that dream happen.

They do not find this hard or stressful because they are pursuing something they enjoy.

Focus on something you enjoy.

Stop spending your time and energy on a job that you hate.

Work in an area you enjoy.

It makes focusing and achieving success easier.

Keep in mind that your time is limited.

Is what you're doing right now moving you towards your goal?

If not stop.

It is crucial that you enjoy your journey.

Start planning some leisure time into your days.

The goal is to remain balanced while you stick to your schedule.

If you focus on nothing, you will receive nothing.

If you do nothing, you will become nothing.

Your focus is everything.

Get specific with your focus to steer your ships in the direction of the solid fertile land you desire.

Aim higher as you focus on bigger and better things.

Why focus on plan b if you believe in plan a?

Why not give all your focus to that?

Stay focused on the best result regardless of the perceived situation.
The world is pliable.
It will mould and change around you based on your thoughts and what you focus on.
Your free will means you are free to focus on what you want and ignore what you don't.

Focus on a future of greatness.
A future where you are healthy, happy, and wealthy.
See the limits as imaginary and watch them break down before you.
Understand that you are powerful and what you think matters in your life.

Become who you want to be,
Not who others think you should be.
This shift is one of the quickest roads to happiness.

When you focus on what you love,
You draw more of it into our lives.
You will become happier.
You must focus on a future that makes you and your family happy.
You must stay steadfast with an unwavering faith and focus on that result.
Because with faith and focus anything is possible.

Chapter 6:

Don't Stay At Home

Today we're going to talk about why you should consider getting out of your house as much as possible, especially if you need to get work done, or if you have some other important personal projects that requires your undivided attention to complete.

For those that work full-time jobs, we all aspire to one day be able to work from home. We all dream of one day being able to just get up from our beds and walk over to our desks to begin work.

Having tried this myself for the last 4 years, I can safely tell you that staying at home isn't all that amazing as it has been talked up or hyped up to be.

While it may sound nice to be able to work from home, in reality, distractions are tough to avoid, and procrastination is one major killer of productivity at home. Many of us have made our homes the Center of entertainment and relaxation. We buy nice couches, TVs, beds, speakers, etc, and all these items around the house are temptations for us to slack off.

For those who are living with family, or who have pets, their presence could also disrupt our productivity.

Without people around us to motivate us to keep working hard, we tend to just tell ourselves "it's okay I'll just watch this one show and then I'll get back to work", and before we know it, it is 5pm and we haven't done a single thing.

Some people love it, some people hate it, but personally, I much prefer getting my butt out of the house and into a co-working space, a cafe, or a library, where I can visually see other people working hard, which motivates me to stay away from slacking off.

Having been doing regular journaling to measure my productivity, staying at home has always resulted in my worst daily performance no matter how hard I try to make my home environment the most conducive for work. Feeling like taking nap because my bed is right there, or watching a Netflix show on my big screen tv, has always been hard to resist. You will be surprised how many hours you are potentially losing from just indulging in any of these things.

For those who really has no choice but to work from home, either to save money, or because you need to take care of a family member. I would highly suggest that you optimise your environment to give yourself the greatest chance of success.

Dedicate a room that will be made into your study/work room, ensure that there is adequate and bright lighting, and to Keep all possible distractions outside the room. Putting your work desk in your bedroom is the worst thing you can do because you will blur the lines between rest and work if you mix the two things up in one tiny space. Not only will you feel sluggish working from your bedroom, but you might also develop sleep issues as well.

Not staying at home is still your best bet for success. Find a space outside where you can be focused and have the discipline to get yourself there every single day, no matter how tired or lethargic you feel. Once you leave the house, you have already won half the battle in getting your productivity under control.

Chapter 7:

Six Steps To Create A Vision For Your Life

Let me ask you this question, have you ever felt so stuck in where you are? That feeling when you wanna move and be somewhere else because you don't like where you are but you don't know where to go either? That is the worst feeling ever, right?

Creating a vision for your life will save you from being stuck and lost. These visions are the pictures you create about the life that you want to live.

Here are 6 Steps To Start Envisioning Your Future

Step number 1, identify what matters to you. Ask yourself, "what's really important to me?". Is it health? Career? Wealth? Relationships? Passion? Time? It could be a balance of all those things. What legacy would you want to leave in this world? Identifying what truly matters to you and what you really value gives you a destination of where you want to be. Having these in mind, all your plans and decisions will be centered towards your destination.

Next step is thinking ahead, but at the same time, also believing that it is already happening for you right now. Be specific in chasing what you want, don't just simply limit yourself to what you think is socially acceptable. If you limit your choices to what seems to be reasonable, you are disconnecting yourself from your true potentialDon't compromise.. Be as audacious as you want to be, it's your own life anyway! You have all the right to dream as big as you want. Talk as if your dreams are happening right now. When you have this big dream, you won't settle for less just because it is what's available at the moment.

Step number 3, assess and challenge your motives. Ask yourself, "is this the kind of life I wanna live because it is what the society is expecting from me?", "am I doing this because this is what everybody else is doing?" Knowing your real motive towards your visions will help you uncover what your heart really desires. You might even be surprised by what you'll discover within you when you remove all the layers that the world has planted in you.

Next step, be sure that your visions are aligned with a purpose. You don't need to know exactly what your life purpose is, unless you've already figured that out somehow. But your visions should be relevant to how you want your life to be. For example, if your goal is to maintain your mental well-being, your vision might be to live your life peacefully while focusing on the things that truly matter. Your vision should serve you the purpose into making your life as pleasing as you want it.

Step number 5 is to be accountable for your own visions. Don't tie your visions into someone else's hands. Your visions may involve direct impact to others but make sure that your visions are not dependent on other people. Why? Because people, just like the seasons, change. People come and go. The version of the people in your life right now is not how they will be for the rest of their lives. And so are you. Hold these visions in your own hands and make sure you execute it diligently and faithfully.

Last step is to make room for changes. You will grow as a person, that is a fact. You won't have the same exact priorities all through your life. And that's okay. Whatever you want to change into is valid. Your goals and dreams are all valid. Changes are inevitable so don't be afraid if you have to change what's working for you from time to time.

While you are in the process of making your life's visions, be as creative as you can. Although the world is not a wish-granting factory, remember that through your hard work and perseverance, nothing is really impossible. You have everything in you to achieve your goals and live through your visions. You just need to be clear about what you really want or where you wanna be.

Remember that our days in this world are limited. We won't be able to live our lives to the fullest if we are just merely existing or living by default. We are humans. And as humans, we have the power to lead the life we truly desire. Sometimes, we are just one decision away from it.

Chapter 8:

The Power of Breathing To Reset Your Mind

Breathing is something we often take for granted. The breath is always there where we notice or not, keeping us going, and keeping us alive. Without our breath, our hearts will not have enough oxygen and we will die a very agonising death. Yet many of us forget to take the time out of the day to utilise this powerful tool of breathing mindfully to reset our focus, and to calm ourselves down in times of stress and anxiety.

Throughout the way, we are bombarded with things. Work stuff, people stuff, family stuff, and our minds and hearts begin racing and stay elevated throughout the day. Induced by stress hormones, we find ourselves full of cluttered thoughts and our productivity and focus drops as a result. Without clearing all these negative emotions that are bottled up inside us, we may find ourselves stressed out and unable to relax throughout the day, and even at night as we try to go to sleep.

This is where the power of conscious breathing comes into play. We all have the power and choice to take 30 seconds out of our day each time we feel that we need to settle down our emotions and clear our head.

Everytime you feel like things are getting out of control, simply stop whatever you are doing, close your eyes, and focus on breathing through our noise. Notice the breath that goes in and out of your nostrils as you inhale and exhale deeply.

By redirecting our focus to our breaths, we momentarily stop our automatic thoughts and are forced to direct attention to each intentional inhalation and exhalation. This conscious awareness to our breath serves to calm our nerves in times of volatility. If you don't believe it, try it for yourselves right now.

This technique has worked for me time and time again. Everytime i catch myself feeling distracted or unhappy, i would stop whatever i was doing, put on my noise cancelling earphones with the music turned off, and to just sit in complete silence as i focused on my breath. After about a minute or two, i find myself with a clearer head. A cleanse of sorts. And then i would attend to whatever task i was doing before.

This takes practice and awareness to be able to do consistently whenever negative emotions rise up. If you feel something is amiss 10x a day, you can carve out 10x of these deep breathing exercises each day as well. Try it and let me know your results.

Chapter 9:

6 Ways To Define What Is Important In Your Life

In this crazy world that we live in, the course of evolution spirals upward and downward, and the collective humanity has witnessed glorious times and horrific ones. The events around us change minute-to-minute. So much seems out of our control, but we find solace in knowing that one thing remains within our immediate control; taking back ownership and responsibility for ourselves. If life has gotten away from you and you feel overwhelmed, anxious or depressed, then maybe it's time to stop and refocus on what's most important to you and find a way back to what really matters to you.

The idea is to evaluate what you're actually doing with and for yourself, determine if it's even essential to you, and then make the said necessary changes that will best accommodate your needs, interests, and desires. Here are some ways to consider how and on what things you should refocus your attention to determine what is most important in your life.

1. Determine What Things You Value Most

Choose and focus on the things around which you have to structure the life that you want to create. When you consciously make these choices, you are more focused on reminding yourself what things in your life you can't and won't do without. These all represent the backbone of your life. We often forget that people and events play a massive role in shaping up to our lives. They Mold us into what we have become so far and what we are to become in the future. Their support and encouragement in our lives are undeniable. We have to see which people and what events we value the most in our lives and then should keep our focus on them more.

2. Decide What Commitments Are Essential To You

Keeping the above valuable things in mind, evaluate which commitments do you value the most in your life. Commitments are the obligations you enter into willingly and represent your promise to see any relationship/project/contract conclusion steadfastly. Renegotiate your essential commitments, if necessary, but consider completing the existing commitments that you are already obligated to and refuse to take any new ones if you aren't ready. That way, you will focus more and fulfill those commitments first that are more significant to you and your life.

3. Assess The Way You Use Your Time

Most of us have a fixed daily routine, with many fixed activities, habits, and chores. Evaluate which things are absolutely necessary and vital for shaping up your life and yourself daily. Assess the time you spend communicating, how much of your time you spend online, emailing, texting, or on your cell phone. How can you cut back the amount of time spent on these activities to do something more productive? How much time are you spending on TV, radio, reading newspapers and magazines? Consider decreasing your consumption and receive the basic information from a reputable source only once throughout the day. Avoid repetition and redundancy.

4. Get Rid of Any clutter That's In Your Life

Look around you and see, do you need everything you have? Give away anything that you haven't used since the last two years. It could be anything, from selling items to furniture, clothing, shoes, etc. Anything that you no longer need. Someone else can happily use what you haven't all this time. And not just the worldly things; get rid of all the emotional and psychological clutter you have kept aside for so long, and it no longer serves you. We have to get rid of the old things to make room for the new things to come. This will help us reflect on our actual being of who we are and where we are.

5. Spend More Time With People That Matter To You

Evaluate how much quality time you actually spend with your family and close friends. As life evolves, more people will enter into your sphere. These people may fall into different categories of importance in your life, such as acquaintances, colleagues, friends, partners, etc. Our time is precious, so it is wise to use it on those that matter to us the most. It's necessary to sort out our interactions and to assess the meaning of each relationship to us.

6.   Make Time To Be Alone

It all comes down to how much time do you make yourself at the end of the day? What was the last time you spent doing something you're passionate about or what you love doing? Give yourself all the time and permission to express your creativity and make peace with your mind. Take care of your body, spirit, and mind because these are the things that will make you feel alive. Take a walk and look around, reacquaint yourself with all the beauty around you. Make each breath count.

Conclusion

Identifying and understanding your values is a challenging but as well as an essential exercise. Your personal values are a central part of defining who you are and who you want to be. By becoming more aware of these significant factors in your life, you can use them as your best guide in any situation. It's comforting and helpful to rely on your values since most of our life's decisions are based on them.

Chapter 10:

STOP TRYING TO BE PERFECT

We're constantly given new advice on how to improve our lives. Meditate. Exercise. Get a hobby. Fast. Everything you do, from what you eat to how you spend your free time, seems like it can be optimized. Especially in the tech world, we're constantly striving toward making things better, ourselves included. It's no secret that running a startup changes your life. You want to make your company the best it can be: the most efficient, innovative, and market leader. It's not surprising that the drive to improve bleeds into the rest of your life.

But, self-improvement as a goal is ineffective. Are we trying to be perfect? And who defines what perfect is? It's so vague as to be unattainable. What if intermittent fasting makes you irritable? What if trying to fit one more thing in your day causes more stress than meditation alleviates? What if you hate kale? What if the "best" way to do things isn't the best way for you? If a goal is unachievable, what's the point in working towards it? It's true. We'll never reach perfection. At no point will we say, "i've reached the peak of who i can be. I can stop now."

But change will happen whether we control it or not. We, as people, are dynamic creatures. We keep growing and evolving throughout our whole lives. Striving for perfection is setting ourselves up for failure.

But, by looking at our lives through the lens of self-improvement, we can be strategic about how we spend our time and energy. There is no one-size-fits-all solution. To be effective, we have to focus on personalized, specific changes.

Despite what the internet may tell you, it takes more than twenty minutes to change your life. It's a cumulative effect of daily or weekly work over a long period. And progress is not linear. As anyone who has built a company knows, there are peaks and valleys. Feeling like you do not see results can make it difficult to stick with a program.

Sometimes, self-improvement can feel impossible. You don't reach a goal and decide you're the best person you can be. It's an ever-evolving process. This can make the process frustrating. You're never done. It can be helpful to think of self-improvement as a practice more than an outcome, even if you do have specific goals you want to achieve. By trying to find enjoyment in work itself, you're more likely to stick with it in the long term.

For high achievers, self-improvement can feel like one more thing on an already full to-do list. Berating yourself for not sticking with a self-improvement plan can cause you to underestimate your potential, limiting your future development. Self-compassion can help encourage the growth mindset necessary for self-improvement. Self-compassion is treating yourself in the face of failure the way you would a good friend. By showing yourself kindness and understanding, you are investing in your wellbeing.

A growth mindset is a way of thinking in which people see their abilities as improvable rather than fixed. If you see your talents as static, why would you work to improve them? By encouraging a growth mindset, every day becomes a chance to get a little bit better. Perfection may be a myth. We will all always be works in progress. But, if we stay open to new experiences and learning opportunities, we give ourselves room to grow.

Chapter 11:

Do The Painful Things First

There are a lot of secret recipes to be happier; one of them is; seek what's painful first. Sure, this may sound a little ironic, but you will be surprised to know that all scientific research is behind this. Behavioral scientists discovered that one of the most effective ways to create an enjoyable experience is to stack the painful parts of the experience early in the process. For example, if you're a doctor, a lawyer, accountant, etc., it's better to break bad news first and then finish with the good news. This will give the clients a more satisfying experience since you start poorly then end on a solid note instead of starting well and ending badly.

There's a couple of crucial reasons why we should do the painful things first. We know that we have limited willpower during the day, and we also know that the most painful activities or tasks are sometimes the most difficult ones. So if we complete the things we find the most difficult first, we'll be exerting less energy on less complicated activities for the rest of the day. Scientific studies show that our prefrontal cortex (creative part of the brain) is the most active the moment we wake up. At the same time, the analytical parts of our brain (the editing and proofreading parts) become more active as the day goes on.

Another reason to do the painful activities firsthand after you wake up is that you would be freed from all the distractions and tend to do these tasks more quickly. If you delay the complex tasks, it will only come back to bite you. Starting with only one task for a day can be enough, as it could lead you to achieve more of them as time goes by. Things like building a new business, losing weight, or learning a new skill require pain and slow work in the beginning to get momentum. But after some persistence, you will likely see your improvements. Behavioral psychology suggests that we're more likely to lead a happier life if we're making improvements over time. Anthony Robbins once said, "If you're not growing, you're dying."

Making slow but gradual improvements is where persistency comes in. It's going to be painful and frustrating initially, and you won't learn a new language in an instant, or your business won't thrive immediately. But when you decide to sacrifice your short-term pleasure for a future pay-off, you will get to enjoy the long-term benefits over a sustained period. Stop avoiding what's hard; embrace it for your long-term happiness.

Chapter 12:

The Power of Imperfect Starts

When you have a goal — starting a business or eating healthier, or traveling the world — it's easy to look at someone who is already doing it and then try to reverse engineer their strategy. In some cases, this is useful. Learning from the experiences of successful people is a great way to accelerate your learning curve.

But it's equally important to remember that the systems, habits, and strategies that successful people are using today are probably not the same ones they were using when they began their journey. What is optimal for them right now isn't necessarily needed for you to get started. There is a difference between the two.

Let me explain.

What is Optimal vs. What is Needed

Learning from others is great, and I do it all the time myself.

But comparing your current situation to someone already successful can often make you feel like you lack the required resources to get started at all. If you look at their optimal setup, it can be really easy to convince yourself that you need to buy new things or learn new skills or meet new people before you can even take the first step toward your goals.

And usually, that's not true. Here are two examples.

Starting a business. When you're an entrepreneur, it's so easy to get obsessed with optimal. This is especially true at the start. I can remember being convinced that my first website would not succeed without a great logo. After all, every popular website I looked at had a professional logo. I've since learned my lesson. Now my "logo" is just my name, and this is the most popular website I've built.

Eating healthy. Maybe the optimal diet would involve buying beef that is only grass-fed or vegetables that are only organic, or some other super-healthy food strategy. But if you're just trying to make strides in the right direction, why get bogged down in the details? Start small and simply buy another vegetable this week — whether it's organic or not. There will be plenty of time for optimization later.

Avoiding by Optimizing

Claiming that you need to "learn more" or "get all of your ducks in a row" can often be a crutch that prevents you from moving forward on the stuff that matters.

- You can complain that your golf game is suffering because you need new clubs, but the truth is you probably just need two years of practice.

- You can point out how your business mentor is successful because they use XYZ software, but they probably got started without it.

Obsessing about the ultimate strategy, diet, or golf club can be a clever way to prevent yourself from doing hard work.

An imperfect start can always be improved, but obsessing over a perfect plan will never take you anywhere on its own.

Chapter 13:

Being Mentally Strong

Have you ever wondered why your performance in practice versus an actual test is like night and day? Or how you are able to perform so well in a mock situation but just crumble when it comes game time?

It all boils down to our mental strength.

The greatest players in sports all have one thing in common, incredibly strong beliefs in themselves that they can win no matter how difficult the circumstance. Where rivals that have the same playing ability may challenge them, they will always prevail because they know their self-worth and they never once doubt that they will lose even when facing immense external or internal pressure.

Most of us are used to facing pressure from external sources. Whether it be from people around us, online haters, or whoever they may be, that can take a toll on our ability to perform. But the greatest threat is not from those areas... it is from within. The voices in our head telling us that we are not going to win this match, that we are not going to well in this performance, that we should just give up because we are already losing by that much.

It is only when we can crush these voices that we can truly outperform our wildest abilities. Mental strength is something that we can all acquire. We just have to find a way to block out all the negativity and replace them with voices that are encouraging. to believe in ourselves that we can and will overcome any situation that life throws at us.

The next time you notice that doubts start creeping in, you need to snap yourself out of it as quickly as you can, 5 4 3 2 1. Focus on the next point, focus on the next game, focus on the next speech. Don't give yourself the time to think about what went wrong the last time. You are only as good as your present performance, not your past.

I believe that you will achieve wonderful things in life you are able to crush those negative thoughts and enhance your mental strength.

Chapter 14:

<u>Why You've Come Too Far To Quit</u>

Remember the first day of school, when someone bullied you for being too nerdy, or for being too whiny. What did you feel when some called you a Four-eye for wearing glasses? What did you do then? How did you answer them? You didn't! Right? Why?

Because you weren't strong enough then to tackle anyone. Because you didn't have any experience to tell you what to do next.

But your parents told you to stop crying and keep doing your thing and one day, everything will be secondary. So you kept your line, didn't indulge in anything anyone else said and you got through that time.

This is the definition of life. Life is a sequence of events that bully you at every corner. But you cannot give up on life, because someone put a dent on your new car or if someone spilled coffee on your shirt.

Things happen because life happens, and you live your life for the things you want to achieve one day.

You dream because you hope for a better future, and that future is worth living for if you have suffered and felt the pain.

Nothing in this life is easy, but nothing is impossible. It may not be possible for you but at the same moment it might be happening for someone else in the world

You have come this far, to achieve the goals your set. You can't give up now only because you haven't seen it yet.

You breathe every day because you have to. Your success has the same needs! You need to give life everything that you got. Not on some days, but every day because it is not something you do when you feel like it, but you have to because you have to live on your terms. No one can dictate your life but only you.

When you feel like quitting, remember why you started it all. You started it to prove everyone wrong. You started it to shun your haters. You started to bully the bullies.

When you feel like quitting, remember, you have too much to fight for and very little to quit for.

When you get up in the morning, remember what you dreamt of last night. Remember your failures and give yourself a chance to prove yourself wrong.

Quitting is for those who are still the kid they were back then. Quitting is for those who still have the feeling that everything will get better on its own - It never does, and it never will. Only if you quit the quitting attitude and start taking initiative for your ultimate dream.

The best you can be is by the best effort you put into being the protagonist of your story. Become the writer of your story. If you want your story to remain average, remain the same person you were a day before.

If your heart tells you to quit, rev up your heart to do one pick one more step towards your penultimate goal. Dictate your heart how bad do you want it.

If you are still the kid who still thinks that things will happen no matter what I do, believe me, you are wrong. This whole attitude of not trying hard enough to achieve your goals is the biggest thing wrong with an average human. But you are not an average human.

The average human wouldn't have the guts to pursue the dream in the first place. An average human wouldn't dream big in the first place. An average human would have given up on the first setback of life and went down a deep hole, only to avoid the problems. But it never is the solution to anything.

Build the guts to keep going no matter what happens. Life will beat you up at every interval. You might have a big setback after every brief moment of happiness.

You might lose friends, family, and everyone you ever cared for. People who were once standing shoulder to shoulder with you might not even care to say your name if they think you don't need what you are striving for. But they don't have a say in your future. It's you who has everything to care for. Everything to account for. So don't give up only because everyone else gave up on you. You are still alive and trying.

Give yourself every chance, to win. Give your life every chance for it to matter. Avail every stone to keep the bullies away, but not by mirroring the act, but your efforts for your goal and they will bow down one day.

Chapter 15:

How to Learn Faster

Remember the saying, "You are never too old to learn something new"? Believe me, it's not true in any way you understood it.

The most reliable time to learn something new was the time when you were growing up. That was the time when your brain was in its most hyperactive state and could absorb anything you had thrown at it.

You can still learn, but you would have to change your approach to learning.

You won't learn everything, because you don't like everything going on around you. You naturally have an ego to please. So what can you do to boost your learning? Let's simplify the process. When you decide to learn something, take a moment and ask yourself this; "Will this thing make my life better? Will this fulfill my dreams? Will I benefit from it?".

If you can answer all these questions in a positive, you will pounce on the thing and you won't find anyone more motivated than you.

Learning is your brain's capability to process things constructively. If you pick up a career, you won't find it hard to flourish if you are genuinely interested in that particular skill.

Whether it be sports, singing, entrepreneurship, cooking, writing, or anything you want to pursue. Just ask yourself, can you use it to increase your creativity, your passion, your satisfaction. If you can, you will start learning it as if you knew it all along.

Your next step to learning faster would be to improve and excel at what you already have. How can you do that? It's simple yet again!

Ask yourself another question, that; "Why must I do this? Why do I need this?" if you get to answer that, you will find the fastest and effective way to the top yourself without any coaching. Why will this happen on its own? Because now you have found a purpose for your craft and the destination is clear as the bright sun in the sky.

The last but the most important thing to have a head start on your journey of learning is the simplest of them all, but the hardest to opt for. The most important step is to start working towards things.

The flow of learning is from Head to Heart to Hands. You have thought of the things you want to do in your brain. Then you asked your heart if it satisfied you. Now it's time to put your hands to work.

You never learn until you get the chance to experience the world yourself. When you go through a certain event, your brain starts to process the outcomes that could have been, and your heart tells you to give it one more try. Here is the deciding moment. If you listen to your heart right away, you will get on a path of learning that you have never seen before.

What remains now is your will to do what you have decided. And when you get going, you will find the most useful resources immediately. Use your instincts and capitalize your time. Capture every chance with sheer will and belief as if this is your final moment for your dreams to come true.

It doesn't matter if you are not the ace in the pack, it doesn't matter if you are not in your peak physical shape, it doesn't matter if you don't have the money yet. You will someday get all those things only if you had the right skills and the right moment.

For all you know, this moment right now is the most worth it moment. So don't go fishing in other tanks when you have your own aquarium. That aquarium is your body, mind, and soul. All you need is to dive deep with sheer determination and the stars are your limit.

Chapter 16:

Why You Are Amazing

When was the last time you told yourself that you were amazing? Was it last week, last month, last year, or maybe not even once in your life?

As humans, we always seek to gain validation from our peers. We wait to see if something that we did recently warranted praise or commendation. Either from our colleagues, our bosses, our friends, or even our families. And when we don't receive those words that we expect them to, we think that we are unworthy, or that our work just wasn't good enough. That we are lousy and under serving of praise.

With social media and the power of the internet, these feelings have been amplified. For those of us that look at the likes on our Instagram posts or stories, or the number of followers on Tiktok, Facebook, or Snapchat, we allow ourselves to be subjected to the validation of external forces in order to qualify our self-worth. Whether these are strangers who don't know you at all, or whoever they might be, their approval seems to matter the most to us rather than the approval we can choose to give ourselves.

We believe that we always have to up our game in order to seek happiness. Everytime we don't get the likes, we let it affect our mood for the rest of the day or even the week.

Have you ever thought of how wonderful it is if you are your best cheerleader in life? If the only validation you needed to seek was from yourself? That you were proud of the work you put out there, even if the world disagrees, because you know that you have put your heart and soul into the project and that there was nothing else you could have done better in that moment when you were producing that thing?

I am here to tell you that you are amazing because only you have the power to choose to love yourself unconditionally. You have the power to tell yourself that you are amazing. and that you have the power to look into yourself and be proud of how far you came in life. To be amazed by the things that you have done up until this point, things that other people might not have seen, acknowledged, or given credit to you for. But you can give that credit to yourself. To pat yourself on the back and say "I did a great job".

I believe that we all have this ability to look inwards. That we don't need external forces to tell us we are amazing because deep down, we already know we are.

If nobody else in the world loves you, know that I do. I love your courage, your bravery, your resilience, your heart, your soul, your commitment, and your dedication to live out your best life on this earth. Tell yourself each and everyday that you deserve to be loved, and that you are loved.

Go through life fiercely knowing that you don't need to seek happiness, validations, and approval from others. That you have it inside you all along and that is all you need to keep going.

Chapter 17:

5 Ways To Adopt Right Attitude For Success

Being successful is a few elements that require hard work, dedication, and a positive attitude. It requires building your resilience and having a clear idea of your future ahead. Though it might be hard to decide your life forward, a reasonable manner is something that comes naturally to those who are willing to give their all. Adopting a new attitude doesn't always mean to change yourself in a way but, it has more meaning towards changing your mindset to an instinct. That is when you get stressed or overworked is because of an opposing point of view on life.

With success comes a great sense of dealing with things. You become more professional, and you feel the need to achieve more in every aspect. Don't be afraid to be power-hungry. But, it also doesn't mean to be unfair. Try to go for a little more than before, each step ahead. Make your hard work or talent count in every aspect. Make yourself a successful person in a positive manner, so you'll find yourself making the most of yourself. And don't give up on the things you need in life.

1. Generate Pragmatic Impressions

"The first impression is the last impression." It's true that once you've introduced yourself to the person in front of you, there is only a tiny chance that you'll get to introduce yourself again. So, choosing the correct wording while creating an impression is a must. You need to be optimistic about yourself and inform the other person about you in a way that influences them. An impression that leaves an effect on them, so they will willingly meet you again. A person must be kind and helpful towards its inferior and respectful towards their superior. This is one of the main characteristics for a person to be a successful man or woman. And with a negative attitude, the opposite occurs. People are more inclined to work without you. They nearly never consider you to work with them and try to contact you as little as possible. So, a good impression is significant.

2. Be True To Your Words

Choose your wording very carefully, because once said, it can't be taken back. Also, for a successful life, commitment is always an important rule. Be true to what you said to a person. Make them believe that they can trust you comfortably. So, it would be best if you chose your words. Don't commit if you can't perform. False commitment leads to loss of customers and leads to the loss of your impression as a successful worker. Always make sure that you fulfill your commands and promises to your clients and make them satisfied with your performance. It leads to a positive mindset and a dedication to work towards your goal.

3. A Positive Personal Life

Whatever you may be doing in your professional life can impact your personal life too. Creating the right mindset professionally also helps you to keep a positive attitude at home. It allows you to go forward with the proper consultation with your heart. It will make you happier. You'll desire to achieve more in life because you'll be satisfied with your success. It will push to go furthermore. It will drive you towards the passion for desiring more. Hard work and determination will continue to be your support, and you will be content will your heart. By keeping a good attitude, you'll be helping yourself more than helping others.

4. Be Aggressive and Determined

Becoming goal-oriented is one of the main factors evolving success in your life. If you are not determined to do your work, you'll just accept things the way others present you. It will leave you in misery and deeply dissatisfied with yourself. Similarly, you'll tend to do something more your way if you are goal-oriented and not how others want. You'll want to shale everything according to your need, and you become delighted with yourself and the result of your hard work. Always keep a clear view of your next step as it will form you in to your true self. Don't just go with the flow, but try to change it according to your wants and needs.

5. Create Your Master Plan

Indeed, we can't achieve great things with only hard work. We will always need to add a factor or to in our business. But by imagining or strategizing, some plans might be helpful. With hard work and some solid projects, we will get our desired outcome. If not, at least we get something close. And if you chose the wrong option, then the amount of hard work won't matter. You'll never get what you want no matter the hard work. So, always make sure to make plans strategically.

Conclusion

By keeping a positive attitude, you'll not only be helpful to others but to yourself too. Make sure you keep the proper manner—a manner required to be a successful person. Do lots of achievements and try to prove yourself as much as possible. Try keeping a good impact on people around you in everything you do. Have the spirit and courage to achieve great heights. And be sure to make moat of yourself. Consistency is the key.

Chapter 18:

Live A Long, Important Life

Do you think you are more capable to deal with the failure or the regret of not trying at all?

Are you living the life you want or the life everyone else wants for you?

Would you feel good spending your time on entertainment that might not last for long? Or would you feel good feeling like you are growing and have a better self of you to look at in the mirror?

Similarly, would like to live in the present or would you love to work for a better future?

Do you want money to dictate your life or do you want money to follow you where ever you go?

Would you prefer being tired or being broke?

Do you want to spend the rest of your life in this place where you and your parents were born? Or do you won't go around the world and find new possibilities in even the most remote places?

Would you rather risk it all or play it safe?

We are often presented with all these questions in our lifetime. Most people take these questions as a way to enter into your adulthood. The answers to these questions are meant to show you the actual meaning of life.

So what is Life? Life is not your parents, your work, your friends, your events, and your functions. It's within you and around you.

You should learn to live your life to the fullest. You should love to live your life for as long as you can with a happy body and a healthy mind.

A happy and healthy body and mind are important. Because you can only feel secure on a stable platform. You can only wish to stand on a platform where you know you can stay put for a long time.

There is nothing wrong with working eight or nine hours in your daily life. It's not unhealthy or anything. Working is what gives our life a purpose. Working is what keeps us active, moving, and motivated.

We have one life, and we have to make it matter. But the way we chose to do it is what matters the most. Our choices make us who we are rather than our actions.

The life we live is the epitome of our intentions and morals. We can be defined in a single word or a single phrase if we ever try. We don't need to analyze someone else, we just need to see ourselves in the mirror and we might be able to see right across the image.

The day we are able to do that, might be the day we have actually made a worthy human being of ourselves and have fulfilled our destiny.

If you are able to look at yourself and go through your whole life in the blink of an eye and cherish the memories as if you were right there at that moment. Believe me, you have had a long and important life to make you think of it all over again every day.

Chapter 19:

<u>The People You Need in Your Life</u>

We all have friends, the people that are there for us and would be there no matter what. These people don't necessarily need to be different, and these traits might all be in one person. Friends are valuable. You only really ever come across ones that are real. In modern-day society, it's so hard to find friends that want to be your friends rather than just to use you.

Sometimes the few the better, but you need some friends that would guide you along your path. We all need them, and you quite possibly have these traits too. Your friends need you, and you may not even know it.

1.   The Mentor

No matter which area or field they are trying to excel in, the common denominator is that they have clarity about life and know exactly what their goals are. These people can impact you tremendously, helps you get into the winners' mindset, infuse self-belief and confidence in you then you, too, can succeed and accomplish your goals. They act as a stepping stone for you to get through your problems. They are happy for your success and would guide you through the troubles and problems while trying to get there.

2.   Authentic People

You never feel like you have to make pretense around these people. Life can be challenging enough, so having friends that aren't judging you and are being themselves is very important for your well-being. This type of friend allows you to be vulnerable, express your emotion in healthy ways, and helps bring a smile back to your face when you're down.

They help you also show your true self and how you feel. Rather than showing only a particular side of their personality, they open their whole self to you, allowing you to do the same and feel comfortable around them.

3. Optimists

These people are the kind you need, the ones that will encourage you through tough times. They will be there encouraging you, always seeing the best in the situation. Having the ability to see the best in people and will always have an open mind to situations. Everyone needs optimism in their lives, and these people bring that.

"Optimism is essential to achievement, and it is also the foundation of courage and true progress." -Nicholas M. Butler.

4. Brutally Honest People

To have a balanced view of yourself and be aware of your blind spots is important for you. Be around people who would provide authentic feedback and not sugarcoat while giving an honest opinion about you. They will help you be a better version of yourself, rectifying your mistakes, work on your weak spots, and help you grow. These are the people you can hang around to get better, and you will critique yourself but in a good way, helping you find the best version of yourself. Of course, the ones that are just rude should be avoided, and they should still be nice to you but not too nice to the point where they compliment you even when they shouldn't.

Chapter 20:

Are You Trying Too Hard To Be A Perfectionist?

There's a fine line between having an achieving behavior and having a perfectionistic behavior. High achievers can be defined as determined, dedicated individuals who have a strong desire to accomplish important things. On the other hand, perfectionism has a flawed mindset that is driven by the avoidance of failure. True perfectionists don't try to be perfect but rather avoid not being good enough. This avoidance may dictate their behavior, leading to depression, anxiety, eating disorders, and even suicide.

Do you ever find yourself in a loop where you are scared of messing up even the tiniest of things? You keep obsessing over that essay over and over again to get it perfect, or you keep panicking over that outfit to get it right. Perfectionism manifests in many aspects of one's life. The stress of not being prepared or something not working out exactly as planned is perfectionism behavior.

Sure, this process may lead you to your desired outcome, like getting an A on that essay or causing someone in the hall to look twice at you. But the question remains, at what cost? How much did you stress over the smallest aspect of what you were trying to achieve? Was it the success that motivated you, or was it the fear of failure? And most importantly, are you being too hard on yourself?

The answer to all of the above questions is probably yes. We dive into everything so deeply that we forget there is no such thing as a perfect person. We are all full of flaws and mistakes. But still, we tend to strive for perfection, and we are looking to do things perfectly. And when it doesn't work out, it becomes detrimental to our progress and mental health. It would seem rather strange, but it is true that perfectionism can trigger procrastination, as the paralyzing fear that you will fail can stop you in your tracks. It's either if I can't do something perfectly, I shouldn't do it at all, or I have to wait for the perfect time to do this perfectly. This attitude would stop you from trying new things, putting yourself out there, or starting your tasks.

Being hard on yourself for trying to be perfect will worsen your mental health and affect your physical health. The blind pursuit of success can lead to neglect of your health and relationships. Recognize that no matter what the result will be, you have worked hard on your end. Acknowledge the efforts that you've put in reaching your goals. The work you do in achieving your goals is sometimes more important than the achievement itself. Find joy in setting goals rather than being weighed down by obligations.

Most importantly, get over it. Nobody's perfect, and you're no exception. Learn to accept your mistakes and flaws instead of holding yourself accountable for every shortcoming and keeping up your standards impossibly high.

Perfectionism is itself an imperfect way to look at life. Failing isn't the end of the world; and rather, it's the beginning of your success. You shouldn't let it get to you and stop you from pursuing your goals. Learn from the experiences and be kinder to yourself. You deserve it!

Chapter 21:

4 Ways to Deal with Feelings of Inferiority When Comparing to Others

When we're feeling inferior, it's usually a result of comparing ourselves to other people and feeling like we don't measure up. And let's be real, it happens all. The. Damn. Time. You could be scrolling through your Instagram feed, notice a new picture of someone you follow, and think: *Wow, how do they always look so perfect?! No amount of filters will make me look like that!* Or maybe you show up to a party, and you quickly realize you're in a room full of accomplished people with exciting lives, and the thought of introducing yourself sends you into a panic. Suddenly, you're glancing at the door and wondering what your best escape plan is. You could be meeting your partner's family for the first time, and you're worried that you won't fit in or that they'll think you're not good enough. You might feel easily intimidated by other people and constantly obsess over what they think of you, even though it's beyond your control.

Don't worry! We have some coping strategies for you that will help you work through your feelings. Try 'em out and see for yourself!

1. Engage in compassionate self-talk

When we feel inferior, we tend to pick ourselves apart and be hard on ourselves. Don't fall into the trap of being your own worst critic! Instead, build your <u>self-confidence</u> and self-esteem by saying positive things to yourself that resonate with you: *I'm feeling inferior right now, but I know my worth. I'm not defined by my credentials, my possessions, or my appearance. I am whole.*

2. Reach out for support or connect with a friend

Just like the Beatles song goes: *I get by with a little help from my friends!* Reach out to someone you can trust and who will be there for you. You might feel inferior now, but it doesn't mean you have to navigate it alone! Get all of those negative feelings off your chest. Having someone there to validate our feelings can be so helpful!

3. Give yourself a pep talk and utilize a helpful statement

Comparing ourselves to other people just brings down our mood and makes us feel like garbage. Sometimes, we gotta give ourselves a little pep talk to turn those negative thoughts around. *I feel inferior right now, but I can get through this! I'm not the only person who has felt this way, and I won't be the last. Everything is gonna be okay!*

4. Comfort yourself like a friend

If you don't have anyone who can be there for you at this moment, that's okay. You can be there for yourself! Think about how you would want a loved one to comfort you at this moment. Pat yourself on the back, treat yourself to some junk food, cuddle up on the couch with a warm, fuzzy blanket and binge your favorite show on Netflix. Be the friend you need right now!

Chapter 22:

When It Is Time To Let Go and Move On (Career)

Today we're going to talk about a topic that I hope will motivate you to quit that job that you hate or one that you feel that you have nothing more to give anymore.

For the purpose of this video, we will focus mainly on career as I believe many of you may feel as though you are stuck in your job but fear quitting because you are afraid you might not find a better one.

For today's topic, I want to draw attention to a close friend of mine who have had this dilemma for years and still hasn't decided to quit because he is afraid that he might not get hired by someone else.

In the beginning of my friend's career, he was full of excitement in his new job and wanted to do things perfectly. Things went pretty smoothly over the course of the first 2 years, learning new things, meeting new friends, and getting settled into his job that he thought he might stay on for a long time to come seeing that it was the degree that he had pursued in university. However when the 3rd year came along, he started to feel jaded with his job. Everyday he would meet ungrateful and sometimes mean customers who were incredibly self-entitled. They would be rude and he started dreading going to work more and more each day. This aspect of the job wore him down and he started to realise that he wasn't happy at all with his work.

Having had a passion for fitness for a while now, he realized that he felt very alive when he attended fitness classes and enjoyed working out and teaching others how to work out. He would fiddle with the idea of attending a teacher training course that would allow him to be a professional and certified fitness coach.

As his full time job started to become more of a burden, he became more serious about the prospect of switching careers and pursuing a new one entirely. At his job, realized that the company wasn't generous at all with the incentives and gruelling work hours, but he stayed on as he was afraid he wouldn't find another job in this bad economy. The fear was indeed real so he kept delaying trying to quit his job. Before he knew it 3 years more had passed and by this time he full on dreaded every single minute at his job.

It was not until he made that faithful decision one day to send in his resignation letter and to simultaneously pay for the teacher training course to become a fitness instructor did his fortunes start to change for him. The fortunes in this wasn't about money. It was about freedom. It was about growth. And it was about living.

We all know deep in our hearts when it is time to call it quits to something. When we know that there is nothing more that we can possibly give to our job. That no amount of time more could ever fulfill that void in us. That we just simply need to get out and do something different.

You see, life is about change. As we grow, our priorities change, our personalities change, our expectations change, and our passions and our interests change as well. If we stay in one place too long, especially in a field or in something that we have hit a wall at, we will feel stuck, and we will feel dread. We will feel that our time spent is not productive and we end up feeling hopeless and sorry for ourselves.

Instead when we choose to let go, when we choose to call time on something, we open up the doors for time on other ventures, and other adventures. And our world becomes brighter again.

I challenge each and everyone of you to take a leap of faith. You know deep in your hearts when it is time to move on from your current job and find the next thing. If you dont feel like you are growing, or if you feel that you absolutely hate your job because there is no ounce of joy that you can derive from it, move on immediately. Life is too short to be spending 10 hours of your life a day on something that you hate, that sucks the living soul out of you. Give yourself the time and space to explore, to find some other path for you to take. You will be surprised what might happen when you follow your heart.

Chapter 23:

How To Be A Better Listener

Today we're going to talk about a topic that could potentially help you not only in your relationships, such as with your boyfriend, girlfriend, and best friends, but also in your workplace with your colleagues, peers, and your bosses or understudies.

Why is being a better listener so vital you might ask? It is simple, because as humans, we all want to be heard. And we all want to feel like people are listening to us and understanding us not just on a superficial level, but emotionally as well. We have a desire to share our pains, sorrows, unhappiness, and even happiness and special events with people who are willing to lend a listening ear to us. And we instantly feel connected to the person who is listening to us.

We are given a mouth and two ears for a reason. I know it sounds silly, but I have to repeat again here that we are social creatures, and we try to find connections with people as much as we can. And there is no better way to be connected than with someone who are willing to spend the time to hear us.

Think back to a time when someone actually told u, thanks for listening to my problems. Either through text or in person. How did you feel? And how did they react to you being a good listener? Were they appreciative?

Or were they nonchalant about it. I would bet that they were appreciative and they know that they had found someone that they could count on to tell their problems too. Of course u dont want it to be a habit that someone constantly "bitches" to you about every single thing that is going wrong in their life. You have to learn how to draw the line there. But generally if it is a one-off problem, I'm sure you guys became better friends, partners, or lovers.

Now think back to a time when someone told u off for not listening to their problems. Where you constantly interjected their sharing with advice without letting them finish what they had to say. This would most likely be your partner who would get angry at you, but what were their feelings at that point? Did they say "you're not listening to me" or "You dont understand?". That has happened to me before on multiple occasions when i tried to impose my ideas on a situation thinking that that is what the person wanted, advice. But in reality, they know how to solve the problem but they just want someone that they could vent to. To share their story and then move on.

So if people have been telling u that you're not a good listener, or that you don't listen or that u dont understand what they want, more often than not, the problem is that you did not just let the person say what they wanted to say, to have their piece. Your job is not to dish out advice, but just to sit there, interested, and ask them to go on. And at the end of it give out a hug rather than an advice.

So you must be wondering how this could link to your colleagues. Well for one, you have to be a good person to begin with in order for people to trust u with work related matters. If colleagues don't trust you, they won't be open to sharing with you problems they might have with their bosses or other issues that they need to vent about. But if they do trust you, and know you are not the type who will go round spreading gossip but rather is a good genuine person with a good heart and a listening ear, you have just gotten yourself an ally at the workplace. And you would have built a friendship at work that could last you a lifetime. You never know when these connections that you have made would provide you with future job opportunities, whether these colleagues could become your bosses in another company one day. But you want to keep your colleagues close to you and you want to retain their respect, trust, and be professional. Vice versa, you may also find a listening ear in a colleague that you can share your problems with. But I must warn you that sometimes people can be disingenuous so you've gotta be careful to not overshare information that could be used against you. Especially through messages where they can be screen captured and could get you in trouble.

On the flip side, Now I want you to use this power for good and not as insider information to manipulate your way up to corporate ladder, do what you will with your gift but karma does come around. And if you have ill intentions for being a good listener, it will come back to bite you someday. I am certain of it. People will know you are a faker and your reputation will precede you.

As you can clearly, being a good listener has immense pay offs for your personal and professional career. And learning to have an open ear could help you gain many potential friends at work and at play. How you respond when people share their stories and having a good character yourself personally also plays an important role in actually keeping these friends close to you as well, but being a good listener is a nice way to start.

Chapter 24:

7 Ways To Remove Excess Noise In Your Life

Ever felt lost in a world that is so fast-paced, where no two moments are the same? Do you ever have a hard time achieving your goals, just because you have more distractions than a purpose to jump to success?

We live in a time, where technology is the biggest ease as well as the biggest difficulty while achieving our goals.

When you need something to be fixed, the internet can save us a lot of time, but the same internet can prove to be the biggest cause to take away the focus of the most determined too.

Although there are many important things on the internet too, that are essential to our daily lives, we don't need them at all times. Especially the realm of social media platforms.

Youtube, Facebook even Instagram can prove to be a beneficial tool for learning and teaching. But it can also make you spend more and more time on things that won't give you much except a good laugh here and there.

So what habits or activities can you adapt to distill these distractions. Reduce noise in life helping you focus better on the things that matter the most.

1. Divide your Tasks Into Smaller Ones

When you already have many distractions in life, including the household tasks and other daily life chores that you must attend to, then you must not avoid those.

But your dreams and goals must not be put aside at all, instead one must learn to complete them by dividing them into smaller, more manageable tasks.

Those who depend on you must have you when they need you, but that shouldn't stop you from doing what you require from yourself.

That can be done by keeping your head in the work whenever you get the chance to get maximum results from those short intervals.

2. Manage Your Time Smartly

Life is too short to be indulging in every whim and activity that you crave. Not everything or thought requires you to act upon.

A human being is the smartest being on this planet but also the stupidest. When a man or a woman wants to achieve something with all their heart, they do get it eventually. But when they have a thousand silly desires to go for, they slide off the set path as if there were none.

"You only Live Once".

Logically, this is a valid quote to get anyone off their path to success. But, realistically this is also the most common reason for the failure of a majority of our youngsters.

You only get this life once, So you must go for the acts that bring you a better future with a surety of freedom without having to rely on anyone. Life doesn't need to be a continuous struggle once you use your energies at the right time for the right time.

3. Get Your Head Out of Social Media

I know this may sound a little Grownup and cliched, but we spend more time on our mobiles and laptops than going out and doing something physically in all our senses with our actual hands.

We can believe and act on anything that pops up on this screen but rarely do we get anything worthwhile that we can adapt to change our lives once and for all.

Social media might be the new medium and source of knowledge and business for many, but for a layman, this is also the biggest waste of creative energy.

There is a lot out there to do in real life, a lot that we can realistically achieve. But, these days, we tend to hide behind a simple tweet and believe that we have done enough when the reality could have been much different.

4. Avoid Unhealthy Relationships

You might have always heard that a friend can be an emotional escape when you need one, but the excess of friends can prove to be the opposite of that. People seem to think, the more friends you have, the better you have a chance to stay engaged and have a happy social life. But this isn't always the case.

The more you have friends, your devotion gets scattered and you find solace in everyone's company. This makes you more exposed, and people might take advantage of that. The fewer friends you have, the better loyalty you can expect and better returns of a favor.

When you have fewer friends, even if you lose one someday or get deceived, you would require less time to bounce back from the incident and you won't have to worry for long.

5. Get Out of Home Environment

Productivity required a productive environment. People tend to look for ease, but it doesn't always help us with finding our true potential.

You sometimes need a strict office environment or a more organized station or workplace. A place where there is no distraction or source of wandering thoughts to get your attention.

People need to understand how our brains work. If you cannot focus sitting in your bed, get a chair and a table. If that doesn't work for you, take a stool without a backrest. If you still feel at ease, just pick a standing table and start working while standing on your feet.

This makes your mind stay more focused on the task at hand to be done quickly.

6.   Make A Schedule For These Distractions

If you feel like you can't give up the urge to pick your phone and check your feed. Or if you need to watch the last quarter of the league, Or if you need to have a smoke.

Don't start fighting these urges. It won't help you, rather make things worse.

If you cannot let go off of these things, it's fine. Make a deal with your brain, that you need this last page done within the next 10 minutes, and then I can go do what I needed direly.

You have to come at peace with your mind and work as a single unit. So make time for these distractions and gradually you might be able to drop them once and for all.

7. You Don't Have to Compare With Anyone

Why do we humans need to compare and compete? Because we think it keeps our drive and our struggle alive. We think it gives us a reason and a purpose to go on and makes us see our goals more clearly.

Comparing to others won't make you see 'Your Goals', rather you would start creating goals that were never meant to be for you. You have these priorities just because you saw someone with something that appealed to you.

This is the noise and distraction that deviates you from the path that was meant to be for you all along.

If you want a clear vision of what you want, start removing cluttered thoughts, acts, and people from your life. It might seem hard at the start, but you won't have any regrets once everything comes in place.

Chapter 25:

Only Buying Things that serve a purpose For you

Today I'm going to talk about the right way to buy things. The right way to shop. The right way to spend your hard earned money.

You see, many of us think that we need to buy things to make working hard at our jobs worth the effort. Sure it does help, in the form of retail therapy for some, but a lot of times we end up just excessively buying things that clutter up our house, our space, our homes. Stuff that we only use once and never touch again. Clothes is a common way that this kind of hoarding happens. We don't notice it because we are buying one shirt or one pants at a time, but over just a few shopping sprees and we find our closets full to the brim. And we never wear some of these clothing's more than once, but we throw the "old" ones to make way for the new.

I believe that the right way to buy things is only to purchase quality items that truly deserve a spot in our homes. Things that bring us joy. Things that we are 1000% sure we will use regularly.

For me, I love apple products. I admit that this one area is where I spend most of my money. I may not buy clothes, shoes, bags, but i will definitely put down money to buy apple products. The thing though is that I only buy items that serve a purpose for me in everyday things that I do. As a music lover, i loved their audio products and the ease of which I can enjoy my favourite music and tv shows with their devices. And I use these products on a daily basis. Everytime i pick up an apple product, i find it such a joy to use.

If you get that same feeling with a particular item, it is okay to get it. I'm not here to tell you u shouldnt be buying anything. As long as it is within your means and you know it will not end up untouched for months, then by all means get it. If something doesn't serve you anymore, sell it, donate it away, keep your space free of clutter.

A clutter-free home can provide enormous benefits for our mental and emotional health. To quote Marie Kondo, and to go one step further, only buy things that truly spark joy in you. Never buy things just because. You may feel good in the moment to splurge, but that feeling won't last. Pick your battles and pick your items carefully.

Chapter 26:

Blaming Others In Your Life For Your Mistakes

When something goes wrong, are you more likely to own up to the mistakes you made, or play the blame game?

Many people are quick to point fingers and play the blame game. In fact, recent research has shown that we *expect* this behavior to happen. We expect to experience others engaging in blame-shifting, placing the blame on others for their own mistakes.

My hands aren't clean. I've blamed people for my own mistakes more than once, that's for sure. Why? It's easy.

Simply put, it's much easier to place the blame on someone else than to take full responsibility for your actions. It's also easier to blame someone for our actions rather than take a deeper look at why we made the mistake that we did and face possible consequences — whether it was something you did at work or something that happened during a tiff between you and your partner. Blame shifting takes less effort, and it's easier on us emotionally — at least in the moment.

"Blame is like another defense mechanism,". "We could call it denial or projection, because it helps us preserve our sense of self-esteem or pride by avoiding awareness of our own issues."

Why do we use defense mechanisms? To protect ourselves — whether it's from criticism, negative consequences, attention, whatever it is you're afraid of. You might even be in denial that you are, in fact, the one who's making mistakes.

"We can think of it as a tool we use when we're in attack mode,".
Alternatively, she notes that some people blame others in an attempt to
hurt them — which is certainly not cool!

Furthermore, it's possible that you might have some deep rooted
negative experiences from your childhood that make you predisposed
to acting in this way. "Psychologically, we can also see that attachment
issues can create problems that manifest when we grow up,". "Insecure
and ambivalent attachments can lead to us not accepting responsibilities
and finding blaming easier."

Seldom does blaming others for our mistakes come without
consequences. It might feel like we're winning in the moment,
benefitting ourselves when we don't take responsibility for our actions,
but that's definitely not the case in the long run. Blaming others can,
and likely will, backfire on you, leaving you wishing you never played
the blame game in the first place.

If it wasn't obvious, those you blame *will* realize it, and they're not
going to be happy that you're not owning up to your own blunders.
As with many toxic behaviors, acknowledging that you have the
problem is the first step to addressing it. Even acknowledging it might
not be easy for you, since finally, you'll have to take the blame yourself,
and hold yourself accountable for your actions. If you're a chronic
blamer, it might have been a while since you took responsibility for
yourself.

We have to learn to be able to hold ourselves accountable for mistakes
big and small, even though it can be scary. It's not easy to own up to
our errors, but without a doubt, it's the right thing to do.

Chapter 27:

Saying Yes To Things

Today we're going to talk about why saying yes can be a great thing for you and why you should do so especially in social invites.

Life you see is a funny thing. As humans, we tend to see things one dimensionally. And we tend to think that we have a long life ahead of us. We tend to take things for granted. We think we will have time to really have fun and relax after we have retired and so we should spend all our efforts and energy into building a career right now, prioritising it above all else. When faced with a choice between work and play, sometimes many of us, including myself choose work over social invites.

There were periods in my life that i routinely chose work over events that it became such a habit to say no. Especially as an entrepreneur, the interaction between colleagues or being in social events is almost reduced to zero. It became very easy and comfortable to live in this bubble where my one and only priority in life is to work work work. 24 hours, 7 days a week. Of course, in reality a lot of time was wasted on social media and Netflix, but u know, at least i could sort of pretend that i was kind of working all day. And I was sort of being productive and sort of working towards my goals rather than "wasting time on social events". That was what I told myself anyway.

But life does not work that way. As I prioritised work over all else, soon all the social invite offers started drying up. My constant "nos" were becoming evident to my social circle and I was being listed as perpetually unavailable or uninterested in vesting time or energy into any friendships or relationships. And as i retreated deeper and deeper into this black hole of "working remotely" i found myself completely isolated from new experiences and meeting new people, or even completely stopped being involved in any of my friend's lives.

I've successfully written myself out of life and I found myself all alone in it.

Instead of investing time into any meaningful relationships, I found that my closest friends were my laptop, tablet, phone, and television. Technology became my primary way of interacting with the world. And I felt connected, yet empty. I was always plugged in to wifi, but i lived my life through a screen instead of my own two eyes. My work and bedroom became a shell of a home that I spent almost all my time, and life just became sort of pointless. And I just felt very alone.

As I started to feel more and more like something was missing, I couldn't quite make out what it was that led me to this feeling. I simply though to myself, hey I'm prioritising work and my career, making money is what the internet tells me I should do, and not having a life is simply part of the price you have to pay... so why am I so incredibly unhappy?

As it turns out, as I hope many of you have already figured out at this point, that life isn't really just about becoming successful financially.

While buying a house, getting a car, and all that good stuff is definitely something that we should strive towards, we should not do so at the expense of our friends. That instead of saying no to them, we should start saying yes, at least once in a while. We need to signal to our friends that hey, yes even though I'm very busy, but I will make an effort to carve out time for you, so that you know I still value you in my life and that you are still a priority.

We need to show our friends that while Monday may not work for us, that I have an opening maybe 2 weeks later if you're still down. That we are still available to grow this friendship.

I came to a point in my life where I knew something had to change. As I started examining my life and the decisions I had made along the way with regards to my career, I knew that what I did wrong was saying no WAAAAAY too often. As I tried to recall when was the last time I actually when I went out with someone other than my one and only BFF, I simply could not. Of the years that went by, I had either said that I was too busy, or even on the off chances that I actually agreed to some sort of meetup, I had the habit of bailing last minute on lunch and dinner appointments with friends. And I never realized that i had such a terrible reputation of being a flaker until I started doing some serious accounting of my life. I had become someone that I absolutely detested without even realising it. I have had people bail on me at the very last minute before, and I hated that feeling. And whenever someone did that to me, I generally found it difficult to ask them out again because I felt that they weren't really that interested in meeting me anyway. That they didn't even bother to reschedule the appointment. And little did I know, I was becoming that very same person and doing the very thing that I hate to my friends. It is no wonder that I started dropping friends like flies with my terrible actions.

As I came to this revelation, I started panicking. It was as if a truck had hit me so hard that I felt that I was in a terrible accident. That how did I let myself get banged up to that extent?

I started scrolling through my contact lists, trying to find friends that might still want to hang out with me. I realized that my WhatsApp was basically dry as a desert, and my calendar was just work for the last 3 years straight with no meaningful highlights, no social events worth noting.

It was at this point that I knew I had made a huge mistake and I needed to change course immediately. Salvaging friendships and prioritising social activities went to the top of my list.

I started creating a list of friends that I had remotely any connection to in the last 5 years and I started asking them out one by one. Some of my friends who i had asked out may not know this, but at that point in my life, i felt pretty desperate and alone and I hung on to every meeting as if my life depended on it. Whilst I did manage to make some appointments and met up with some of them. I soon realized that the damage had been done. That my friends had clearly moved on without me... they had formed their own friends at work and elsewhere, and I was not at all that important to have anymore. It was too little too late at that point and there was not much I could do about it. While I made multiple attempts to ask people out, I did not receive the same offers from people. It felt clearly like a one-way street and I felt that those people that I used to call friends, didn't really see me as one. You see growing a friendship takes time, sometimes years of consistent meetups before this person becomes indispensable in your life. Sharing unique experiences that allow your friends to see that you are truly vested in them and that you care about them and want to spend time with them. I simply did not give myself that chance to be integrated into someone's life in that same way, I did not invest that time to growing those friendships and I paid the price for it.

But I had to learn all these the hard way first before I can receive all the good that was about to come in the future.

Chapter 28:

How to Deal with Stress Head On? 7 Things You Can Start Today

Drop your shoulders, release your tongue from your palate. Unclench your teeth and let your brows relax. You see, this is how stressed you are all the time, you forget completely about how it is affecting your body.

In this roaring river of the 21st century, we are all feeling the tide rising and falling 24/7. It will be a white lie if any of you claim to never feel stressed. We are all under varying degrees of stress all the time.

So what is stress exactly? Stress is not merely a stimulus or a physical response of our bodies but a process by which we appraise and cope with environmental threats and challenges. When expressed in short bursts or taken as a challenge, stressors may have positive effects. However, if stress is threatening or prolonged, it can be harmful for us.

So how then do we handle it?

It seems like quite a drag for most of us and pretty annoying a lot of the time, but here are several ways we can deal with it and come out of it stronger than before.

7 Tips to Deal with stress and anxiety

Number 1: Go To Bed Early and Wake up Early

Have you heard the quote "Early to Bed, early to rise, makes a man healthy, wealthy and wise."? When was the last time you went to sleep early? I believe that going to bed early is something we all know we need to do but hardly ever do.

Starting your day off early has many wonderful biological effects. Mornings tend to be cool, silent, serene, and distraction-free. This calmness helps bring our stress levels down and prepares us for the day ahead. By practicing some deep breathing techniques in the morning, it will also aid in flow and circulation throughout our bodies, something that is good for the mind and soul.

Number 2: Start Practicing Yoga or meditation

Yoga and meditation, while they are two separate practices, they overlap in many key areas. Yoga poses are great for us to engage with our bodies, to stretch out our muscles, tight sections of our bodies, and to help us focus on our breath at all times. Each yoga pose targets a unique meridian of our bodies, many allowing us to release tensions that might otherwise have built up without realizing. You can try simple poses such as a child pose or shavasana, or downward dog, to get yourself started.

Meditation on the other hand focuses stilling the mind through focus on the breath as well. Letting our thoughts flow freely, we are able to acknowledge the stressors we face without judgement. Try out some guided mindfulness meditation practices to get your started.

Number 3: Having Proper Time Management

Many of us overlook the importance of proper time management. We often let our crazy schedules overwhelm us. By being unorganized with our time, we are also unorganized with our emotions. If we let our calendar be filled with chaos, there is no doubt that we will feel like chaos as well. Stress levels will be bound to rise. Have proper blocks of time dedicated to each task in your day. Trust me you will feel a whole lot more in control of everything.

Number 4: Make time for your hobbies

We should all strive to live a happy and balanced life. If work is the only thing on our agenda, we will have no outlet to destress, relax, recharge, and be ready to face new challenges that might tax our physical and mental abilities.

Whatever your hobbies are: baking, tennis, crafting, surfboarding, or even shopping, as long as you plan them in your schedule and do them, you will definitely feel a whole lot better about everything. Let out all the steam, stress, anxieties, as you engage in your hobbies, or even just forget about them for a minute. Give yourself the space to breathe and just enjoy doing the fun things in life. Life isn't just all about work. Play is equally important too.

Number 5: Music is food for your soul

Music has many therapeutic qualities. If you feel your stress levels rising, consider popping your earbuds into your ears and playing your favorite songs on spotify. If you are looking for calm, you may want to consider listening to some chill music as well.

The kind of your music you listen to will have a direct effect on your mood and the way you feel. So choose your playlists wisely. Don't go heavy metal or goth, unless of course it helps calm you down.

Number 6: Start Cleaning your clutter

This may seem like I am quoting a movie where the stressed teenage girl decides to clean her room when she is feeling low. I'd say movies are made out of someone's real experience.

Cleaning your room or clutter can be one of the best therapies.

A messy space is a recipe for anxiety and stress. When we see clutter, we feel cluttered. Once you clear all the stuff you don't need, you will feel much lighter instantly.

Number 7: Allow nature to heal you

Nature is amusing and wonderful. Everything in nature is closer to our basic making than anything that we are dealing with today. So try getting close to nature, it will make you feel relaxed and at the same time enable you to enrich your brain.

Watch the sun setting into the sky and wake up to look at the colors at dawn.
There is nothing more beautiful in this world that we get to experience every single day no matter where we are on this earth.

Take a stroll in your favourite park, go for a cycle, a jog, or even just a stroll with your pet. Allow nature to melt away your stress and bring your peace.

Final Thoughts

Stressors are a part of life. Something we cannot escape from. But if we put in place some healthy habits and practices, we can reduce and release those negativities from our bodies, cleansing us to take on more stress in the future.

Chapter 29:

How to Build Skills That Are Valuable

The most valuable skills you can have in life and work are rarely taught in school, never show up on a resume, and are consistently overlooked and underappreciated. But there's some good news: It costs nothing to develop them, and you have the opportunity to do so.

Here's how

1. The Ability To Pay Attention

The shorter the average attention span gets, the more valuable your ability to focus becomes.

It's a huge competitive advantage to be able to pay attention to things for an extended period (and unfortunately, what passes for an extended period these days may be as little as 10 minutes).

The ability to pay attention helps you learn, communicate, be productive, and see opportunities others miss, among countless other things.

Two ways to improve your ability to pay attention:

- Practice single-tasking — read a book, watch a movie, or find some other thing to do for an extensive amount of time without allowing yourself to do anything else during that time. No side conversations. No checking your phone. Nothing but focus on that one thing.

- Become intentional with how you use your phone (and for the love of God, turn off your notifications!).

2. The Ability To Follow Directions

This one takes your improved ability to pay attention a step further.

Every aspect of your life and career involves directions —customers tell you what they want, your boss tells you what she needs to be done, and the people you care about tell you what they expect of you.

It's one thing to pay attention to instructions, but it's another to accurately follow them.

The best qualifications in the world won't land you a job if your application doesn't include the employer's requested details.

Your company won't care about your innovative ideas if they don't align with the problems they asked you to solve.

And the reason Facebook Ads may not work for you isn't that Facebook ads don't work — it's because you don't know the right ways to use them.

The ability to follow directions serves as a filter that keeps otherwise qualified people from succeeding — and most of them don't even realize their struggles are rooted in this weakness.

Don't let that be you.

Two ways to improve your ability to follow directions:

1. Ask for directions on how to do things more often. Practice makes perfect.
2. Give directions to other people. Take something you know how to do (like write a blog post, for example), and write up directions to help others do it the way you do (like I did here). Teaching is a great

way to learn, and the process of creating directions will help you recognize the importance of little steps in directions you get from others.

The point of this post isn't to make you feel overwhelmed. The truth is, you already have these skills — we all do. But I wrote this because I've noticed many people don't think about these abilities as skills and therefore don't do much to hone them.

Chapter 30:

8 Tips to Become More Resilient

Resilience shows how well you can deal with the problems life throws at you and how you bounce back. It also means whether you maintain a positive outlook and cope with stress effectively or lose your cool. Although some people are naturally resilient, research shows that these behaviors can be learned. So, whether you are going through a tough time right now or you want to be prepared for the next step in your life, here are eight techniques you can focus on to become more resilient.

1. Find a Sense of Purpose

When you are going through a crisis or a tragedy, you must find a sense of purpose for yourself; this can play an important role in your recovery. This can mean getting involved in your community and participating in activities that are meaningful to you so every day you would have something to look forward to, and your mind wouldn't be focusing on the tragedy solely. You will be able to get through the day.

2. Believe in Your Abilities

When you have confidence in yourself that you can cope with the issues in your life, it will play an important role in resilience; once you become confident in your abilities, it will be easier for you to respond and deal with a crisis. Listen to the negative comments in your head, and once you do, you need to practice replacing them with positive comments like I'm good at my job, I can do this, I am a great friend/partner/parent.

3. Develop a Strong Social Network

It is very important to be surrounded by people you can talk to and confide in. When you have caring and supportive people around you during a crisis, they act as your protectors and make that time easier for you. When you are simply talking about your problems with a friend or a family member, it will, of course, not make your problem go away. Still, it allows you to share your feelings and get supportive feedback, and you might even be able to come up with possible solutions to your problems.

4. Embrace Change

An essential part of resilience is flexibility, and you can achieve that by learning how to be more adaptable. You'll be better equipped to respond to a life crisis when you know this. When a person is resilient, they use such events as opportunities to branch out in new directions. However, it is very likely for some individuals to get crushed by abrupt changes, but when it comes to resilient individuals, they adapt to changes and thrive.

5. Be Optimistic

It is difficult to stay optimistic when you are going through a dark period in your life, but an important part of resilience can maintain a hopeful outlook. What you are dealing with can be extremely difficult, but what will help you is maintaining a positive outlook about a brighter future. Now, positive thinking certainly does not mean that you ignore your problem to focus on the positive outcomes. This simply means understanding that setbacks don't always stay there and that you certainly have the skills and abilities to fight the challenges thrown at you.

6. Nurture Yourself

When you are under stress, it is easy not to take care of your needs. You can lose your appetite, ignore exercise, not get enough sleep. These are all very common reactions when you are stressed or are in a situation of crisis. That is why it is important to invest time in yourself, build yourself, and make time for activities you enjoy.

7. Develop Problem-Solving Skills

Research shows that when people are able to come up with solutions to a problem, it is easier for them to cope with problems compared to those who can not. So, whenever you encounter a new challenge, try making a list of potential ways you will be able to solve that problem. You can experiment with different strategies and eventually focus on developing a logical way to work through those problems. By practicing your problem-solving skills on a regular basis, you will be better prepared to cope when a serious challenge emerges.

8. Establish Goals

Crisis situations can be daunting, and they also seem insurmountable but resilient people can view these situations in a realistic way and set reasonable goals to deal with problems. So, when you are overwhelmed by a situation, take a step back and simply assess what is before you and then brainstorm possible solutions to that problem and then break them down into manageable steps.

Chapter 31:

6 Steps To Get Out of Your Comfort Zone

The year 2020 and 2021 have made a drastic change in all our lives, which might have its effect forever. The conditions of last year and a half have made a certain lifestyle choice for everyone, without having a say in it for us.

This new lifestyle has been a bit overwhelming for some and some started feeling lucky. Most of us feel comfortable working from home, and taking online classes while others want to have some access to public places like parks and restaurants.

But the pandemic has affected everyone more than once. And now we are all getting used to this relatively new experience of doing everything from home. Getting up every day to the same routine and the same environment sometimes takes us way back on our physical and mental development and creativity.

So one must learn to leave the comfort zone and keep themselves proactive. Here are some ways anyone can become more productive and efficient.

Everyone is always getting ready to change but never changing.

1. Remember your Teenage Self

People often feel nostalgic remembering those days of carelessness when they were kids and so oblivious in that teenage. But, little do they take for inspiration or motivation from those times. When you feel down, or when you don't feel like having the energy for something, just consider your teenage self at that time.

If only you were a teenager now, you won't be feeling lethargic or less motivated. Rather you'd be pushing harder and harder every second to get the job done as quickly as possible. If you could do it back then, you still can! All you need is some perspective and a medium to compare to.

2. Delegate or Mentor someone

Have you ever needed to have someone who could provide you some guidance or help with a problem that you have had for some time?

I'm sure, you weren't always a self-made man or a woman. Somewhere along the way, there was someone who gave you the golden quote that changed you consciously or subconsciously.

Now is the time for you to do the same for someone else. You could be a teacher, a speaker, or even a mentor who doesn't have any favors to ask in return. Once you get the real taste of soothing someone else's pain, you won't hesitate the next time.

This feeling of righteousness creates a chain reaction that always pushes you to get up and do good for anyone who could need you.

3. Volunteer in groups

The work of volunteering may seem pointless or philanthropic. But the purpose for you to do it should be the respect that you might get, but the stride to get up on your feet and help others to be better off.

Volunteering for flood victims, earthquake affectees or the starving people of deserts and alpines can help you understand the better purpose of your existence. This keeps the engine of life running.

4. Try New Things for a Change

Remember the time in Pre-school when your teachers got you to try drawing, singing, acting, sculpting, sketching, and costume parties. Those weren't some childish approach to keep you engaged, but a planned system to get your real talents and skills to come out.

We are never too old to learn something new. Our passions are unlimited just as our dreams are. We only need a push to keep discovering the new horizons of our creative selves.

New things lead to new people who lead to new places which might lead to new possibilities. This is the circle of life and life is ironic enough to rarely repeat the same thing again.

You never know which stone might lead you to a gold mine. So never stop discovering and experiencing because this is what makes us the supreme being.

5. Push Your Physical Limits

This may sound cliched, but it always is the most important point of them all. You can never get out of your comfort zone, till you see the world through the hard glass.

The world is always softer on one side, but the image on the other side is far from reality. You can't expect to get paid equally to the person who works 12 hours a day in a large office of hundreds of employees. Only if you have the luxury of being the boss of the office.

You must push yourself to search for opportunities at every corner. Life has always more and better to offer at each stop, you just have to choose a stop.

6. Face Your Fears Once and For All

People seem to have a list of Dos and Dont's. The latter part is mostly because of a fear or a vacant thought that it might lead to failure for several reasons.

You need a "Do it all" behavior in life to have an optimistic approach to everything that comes in your way.

What is the biggest most horrible thing that can happen if you do any one of these things on your list? You need to have a clear vision of the possible worst outcome.

If you have a clear image of what you might lose, now must try to go for that thing and remove your fear once and for all. Unless you have something as important as your life to lose, you have nothing to fear from anything.

No one can force you to directly go skydiving if you are scared of heights. But you can start with baby steps, and then, maybe, later on in life you dare to take a leap of faith.

"Life is a rainbow, you might like one color and hate the other. But that doesn't make it ugly, only less tempting".

All you need is to be patient and content with what you have today, here, right now. But, you should never stop aiming for more. And you certainly shouldn't regret it if you can't have or don't have it now.

People try to find their week spots and frown upon those moments of hard luck. What they don't realize is, that the time they wasted crying for what is in the past, could have been well spent for a far better future they could cherish for generations to come.

Chapter 32:

Six Habits of Self-Love

We can show gratitude to ourselves for our different achievements in many ways. It is something that most people overlook as a waste of time and resources. This is a fallacy. It is high time we develop habits of self-love, to recharge our bodies and minds in preparation for another phase of achievements.

Here are six habits of self-love:

1. Treating Yourself

It is showing gratitude to yourself by way of satisfying your deepest desires instead of waiting for someone else to do it for you. Take the personal initiative to go shopping and buy that designer suit or dress you have been wanting so badly. Do not wait for someone else to do it for you while you are capable.

Take that much-needed vacation and a break from work to be with your family. Spend time with the people you love and cherish every moment because, in this fast-moving world, the future is uncertain. Secure your happiness lest you drown in depression. The best person to take care of your interests is yourself.

Who will take you out for swimming or outing to those posh hotels if you do not initiate it? Self-love begins when you realize your worth and do not allow anyone else to bring it down.

2. Celebrate Your Victories

Take advantage of every opportunity to celebrate your wins, no matter how small. A habit of self-love is to celebrate your achievements and ignore voices that discourage you. Nothing should muffle you from shouting your victories to the world. The testimony of your victory will encourage a stranger not to give up in his/her quest.

It is neither pride nor boastfulness. It is congratulating yourself for the wins that you rightfully deserve. How else can you love yourself if you do not appreciate yourself for the milestones you have conquered? Do not shy away from thanking yourself, privately or publicly, because no one else best knows your struggles except yourself.

3. Accept Yourself

To begin with, accept your social and economic status because you know the battles you have fought. Self-acceptance is an underrated form of self-love. Love yourself and accept your shortcomings. When you learn to accept yourself, other people will in turn accept you. They will learn how to accommodate you in the same manner you learned to live with all your imperfections.

Self-loathing dies when you master self-acceptance and self-love. Self-care keeps off self-rejection. You begin seeing your worth and great potential. It is the enemy within that is responsible for the fall of great empires.

The enemy within is low self-esteem and self-rejection. Accept the things you cannot change and change the things in your ability. Do not be hard on yourself because a journey of a thousand miles begins with a single step.

4. Practice Forgiveness

Forgiveness is a strong act. When you forgive those who wrong you, you let go of unnecessary baggage. It is unhealthy to live with a heart full of hate (pun intended). Forgiveness does not mean that you have allowed other people to wrong you repetitively. It means you have outgrown their wrong acts and you no longer allow their inconsiderate acts to affect you. Forgiveness benefits the forgiver more than the forgiven. It heals the heart from any hurt caused. It is the best form of self-care yet difficult at the same time. Forgiveness is a gradual process initiated by the bigger person in any conflict. Practicing self-care is by recognizing the importance of turning a new leaf and staying free from shackles of grudges and bitterness.

Unforgiveness builds bitterness and vengeance. It finally clouds your judgment and you become irrational. Choosing forgiveness is a vote on self-care.

5. Choose Your Associates Wisely

Associate with progressive people. Show me your friends and I will tell you the kind of person you are. Your friends have the potential to either build or destroy your appreciation of self-worth. They will trim your excesses and supplement your deficiencies. A cadre of professionals tends to share several traits.

Self-care involves taking care of your mental state and being selective of who you let into your personal space. It supersedes all other interests.

6. Engaging In Hobbies

Hobbies are the activities we do during our free time to relax our minds and bond with our friends. When doing these hobbies we are at ease and free from pressures of whatever form. We need to take a break from our daily work routine from time to time and do other social activities.

Hobbies are essential to explore other interests and rejuvenate our psyche and morale. Self-love places your interests and well-being above everything else. There is a thin line between it and selfishness, but it is not the latter.

These six habits of self-love will ensure you have peace and sobriety of mind to make progressive decisions.

Chapter 33:

Five Habits of A Healthy Lifestyle

A healthy lifestyle is everybody's dream. The young and old, rich and poor, weak and strong, and male and female all want a happily ever after and many years full of life. The price to pay to achieve this dream is what distinguishes all these classes of people. What are you ready to forego as the opportunity cost to have a healthy lifestyle?

Here are five habits for a healthy lifestyle.

1. Eating Healthy Food

Your health is heavily dependent on your diet. You have heard that what goes inside a man does not defile him, but what goes out of him does. In this case, the opposite is true. What a man takes as food or beverage affects him directly. It can alter the body's metabolism and introduce toxins in the body hence endangering his life.

Most people do not take care of what they feed on. They eat anything edible that is readily available without any consideration. All other factors like the nutritive value of the food and its hygiene are secondary to most modern people who have thrown caution to the wind. Towns and cities are full of fast food joints and attract masses from all over. It is the most lucrative business these days. Are these fast foods healthy?

As much as the hygiene could be up to standards (due to the measures put in place by authorities), the composition of these foods (mostly chips and broiler chicken) is wanting. The cooking oil used is full of cholesterol that is a major cause of cardiac diseases. To lead a healthy lifestyle, eating healthy food should be a priority.

2. Regular Exercising

The human body requires regular exercise to be fit. Running, walking, swimming, or going to the gym are a few of the many ways that people can exercise. It is a call to get out of your comfort zone to ward off some lifestyle diseases. It is often misconstrued that exercising is a reserve for sportsmen and women. This fallacy has taken root in the minds of many people.

Unlearn the myths about exercises that have made most people shun them. The benefits of exercising are uncountable. It improves pressure and blood circulation in the body. Exercises also burn excess calories in tissues that would otherwise clog blood vessels and pose a health hazard. Research has shown that most people who exercise are healthy and fall sick less often. This is everyone's dream but the few who choose to pay the price enjoy it. Choose to be healthy by doing away with frequent motor vehicle transport and instead walk. A simple walk is an exercise already. When you fail to exercise early enough, you will be a frequent patient at the hospital. Prevention is always better than cure.

In the words of world marathon champion, Eliud Kipchoge, a running nation is a healthy nation.

3. Regular Medical Checkup

When was the last time you went for a medical checkup even when you were not sick? If the answer is negative or a long time ago, then a healthy lifestyle is still unreachable. A medical examination will reveal any disease in its early stages.

In most third-world countries, healthcare systems are not fully developed. Its citizens only go to the hospital when a disease has progressed and is in its late stages. At such a time, there is a higher probability of the patient succumbing to it. Doctors advise people to seek medical attention at the slightest symptom to treat and manage long-term illnesses. Regular medical checkups help one become more productive at work.

Is a healthy lifestyle attainable? Yes, it is when one takes the necessary measures to fight diseases. Regular medical checkups can be financially draining. Seek an insurance policy that can underwrite your health risks and this will make medical expenses affordable.

4. Staying Positive

A bad attitude is like a flat tire. If you do not change it, you will never go anywhere. There is a hidden power in having a positive attitude towards life. It all starts in the mind. When you conceive the right attitude towards life, you have won half the battle.

A healthy lifestyle starts with the mind. If you believe it, you can achieve it. So limitless is the human mind that it strongly influences the direction of a person's life. As much as there are challenges in life, do not allow them to conquer your mind or take over your spirit. Once they do, you will be constantly waging a losing battle. Is that what we want?

Associate with positive like-minded people and you will be miles away from depression and low self-esteem. We all desire that healthy lifestyle.

5. Have A Confidant And A Best Friend

Who is a best friend? He/she is someone you can trust to share your joy and sadness, and your high and low moments. You should be careful in your selection of a confidant because it may have strong ramifications if the friendship is not genuine.

A confidant is someone you can confide in comfortably without fear of him/her leaking your secrets. He/she will help you overcome some difficult situations in life. We all need a shoulder to lean on in our darkest times and a voice to comfort us that it is darkest before dawn. This helps fortify our mental health. We grow better and stronger in this healthy lifestyle.

These are the five habits for a healthy lifestyle. When we live by them, success becomes our portion.

Chapter 34:

Dealing With Addiction To Technology

Today we're going to talk about addiction to technology and media consumption. I think this is a topic that many of us can relate, even myself included. Am my goal for today is to try to help put forth a more sustainable and healthy habit for you to still enjoy technology while not being overwhelmed and overtaken by it completely.

So lets ask ourselves a simple question of why are we so hooked into using our devices so frequently and sparingly? I think for most of us, and this is my personal opinion, is that it offers us an escape, a distraction from our every day tasks that we know we ought to do. To procrastinate just a little bit or to binge scroll on Instagram, Facebook, Snapchat, and what have you, to satisfy our need for media consumption.

We use technology as a tool a gateway into the world of digital media, and we get lost in it because companies try to feed us with posts and stuff that we like to keep us engaged and to keep us watching just a little while longer. And minutes can turn into hours, and before you know it, it is bedtime.

I want to argue that this addiction is not entirely your fault, but that these multi-billion dollar mega companies are being fed so much data that they are able to manipulate us into consume their media. It is like how casinos use various tricks of flickering lights, and free drinks to keep you playing a little longer and to spend a little more of your attention and time. We unknowingly get subjected to these manipulative tactics and we fall for it despite our best efforts to abstain from it.

I for one have been the subject of such manipulation. Whether it be Netflix or my favourite social media apps, I find myself mindlessly scrolling through posts trying to get my quick fix of distraction and supposed stress relief. However these feelings dont bring me joy, rather it brings me anxiety that I have wasted precious time and I end up kicking myself for it afterwards. This happens time and time again and it felt like I was stuck in a loop, unable to get out.

So what is the solution to this seemingly endless spiral of bad habits? Some might say just to delete the apps, or turn off wifi. But how many of you might have actually tried that yourself only to have it backfire on you? Redownloading the app is only one step away, wifi is only one button away, and addictions aren't so easily kicked to the curb as one might think.

What I have found that works is that instead of consuming mindless media that don't bring about actual benefit to my life, I chose to watch content that I could actually learn something from. Like this channel for example. I went on the hunt to seek out content that I could learn how to make extra money, how to improve my health, how to improve my relationships, basically anything that had to do with personal development. And I found that I actually felt less guilty watching or reading these posts even though they still do take up my time to consume.

You may call it a lesser of two evils, but what I discovered was that it provided much more benefit to my life than actually not consuming any personal development media at all. Whether it be inspirational stories from successful entrepreneurs like Elon Musk, or Jeff Bezos, or multi billion dollar investment advice from Warren Buffet, these passive watching of useful content actually boosted my knowledge in areas that I might otherwise have not been exposed to. Subconsciously, i started internalizing some of these beliefs and adopted it into my own psyche. And i transformed what was mindless binge watching of useless Tv shows and zombie content, to something that actually moved the needle in my life in the right direction, even by a little.

Overtime, I actually required less and less distraction of media consumption using my technology devices like iPhones and iPads or Macs, and started putting more attention and effort to do the work that I knew i had to get done. Because some of these personal development videos actually taught me what I needed to do to get stuff done and to stop procrastinating in working towards my goals.

So I challenge each and everyone of you today to do a thorough review of the kinds of music and media consumption that you consume today with your smartphones and tablets, and see if you can substitute them with something that you can learn from, no matter how trivial you think it may be. It could be the very push you need to start porting over all your bad habits of technology into something that can pay off for you 10 years down the road.